BarCharts, Inc.®

WORLD'S #1 ACADEMIC OUTLINE

Quick Study® ACADEMIC

American History 1

Discovery of New World through Civil War & Reconstruction

The New World 1492-1646

1492 **Christopher Columbus** lands in the Bahamas.

1513 **Ponce de Leon** lands in Florida (FL).

1518 **Smallpox**, brought by the **Europeans**, begins to decimate the native populations of Central and South America. The epidemic will last until 1530.

1521 Surrender of Tenochtitlan (Aztec capital) to **Spanish** explorer/conqueror **Hernando Cortes**; the **Aztec** empire falls.

1533 **Henry VIII** starts the **English Reformation**, mainly to gain a divorce from **Katherine of Aragon**.

1539-1540 **Hernando de Soto** begins exploration of what will be the southeastern United States; **Francisco Vasquez de Coronado** does the same in the Southwest.

1558 Henry VIII's daughter, **Elizabeth**, becomes **Queen Elizabeth (I)** of England.

1584 **1584-90: Sir Walter Raleigh** starts, and fails, with a colony in **Roanoke** (an island off North Carolina [NC]), the first attempt in North America.

1588 **The English Navy**, helped by violent storms, defeats **the Spanish Armada**.

1603 **James I** becomes King of England.

1603-1605 **Samuel de Champlain** of France explores what will be present-day Canada.

1607 **Jamestown (Virginia Colony)** is founded.

1611 The first Virginia (VA) **tobacco** crop is harvested.

1619 The first **African slaves** arrive in VA.

1620 **Plymouth Colony (Massachusetts [MA])** is founded.

1622 **Powhatan Confederacy** attacks the Virginia Colony.

1624 **The Dutch** settle Manhattan Island.

1625 **Charles I** becomes King of England.

1630 **The Massachusetts Bay Colony** is founded.

1634 **Maryland (MD)** is founded as "haven for **English Catholics**."

1635 **Roger Williams** is "expelled" from the Massachusetts Bay Colony, and founds **Providence (Rhode Island [RI])**.

1636 **Connecticut (CT)** is founded.

1637 **The Pequot War** virtually wipes out the **Pequot Indian** tribe.

1646 VA and Powhatan Confederacy sign peace treaty.

A Society Forms 1642-1732

1642-1646 **The English Civil War** sends many in search of the "New World."

1649 **King Charles I (House of Stuart)** is executed.

1660 The House of Stuart returns to the throne of England, and **King Charles II** rules.

1662
1. The *Halfway Covenant* is drafted in MA.
   a. Adults who had been baptized but were not full church members could have their children baptized if they recognized church authority and lived by its precepts.
   b. They could not, however, vote or take communion.

1663 **Carolina** is chartered.

1664 England defeats the Dutch and takes over New Netherland, renaming it **New York (NY)**.

1675
1. **King Philip's War.**
   a. **Chief Metacomet ("King Philip")** of **Pokanet** tribe rises against **Pilgrim** encroachment of tribal lands.
   b. Destroys 12 of 90 Puritan towns.
   c. Lack of food and ammunition brings about defeat.
   d. Metacomet killed. Tribe virtually wiped out, except in Martha's Vineyard area.

1676
1. **Bacon's Rebellion** in VA.
   a. Farmer **Nathaniel Bacon** rouses farmers to fight against government corruption.
   b. **Governor William Berkeley** declares Bacon "in rebellion."
   c. Bacon marches on Jamestown and burns capitol building to the ground. When he dies of dysentery, the rebellion collapses.

1680
1. **Pueblo Revolt.**
   a. Led by medicine man **Pope** (pronounced "po-pay"), **Pueblos** in New Mexico (NM) revolt against **Spaniards** and drive them out.

1680 (cont.)
   b. Spaniards out of power until 1692, when [illegible] engender new spirit of cooperation with [illegible]
2. MD colonists, "forced" to eat the oysters [illegible] their shore to keep from starvation, found a n[illegible]stry.

1681 **Pennsylvania (PA)** is chartered.

1685 **James II** is King of England.

1686
1. **Dominion of New England** is formed.
   a. Charters of all individual states revoked [illegible] **"Non-English"** practices.
   b. **Sir Edmund Andros** is named Gover[illegible] Dominion.

1688 James II is deposed in the **"Glorious R[illegible]"** **William & Mary** gain the throne.

1689
1. Dominion of New England is overthrown.
   a. Andros jailed.
   b. Return to former state charters hoped for but not achieved.
2. **King William's War.**
   a. a.k.a., The **War of the League of Augsburg.**
   b. **Americans** fight on northern frontiers.
   c. Many colonies are decimated.
   d. Ends in 1697.

1692
1. **Salem Witchcraft** hysteria.
   a. Started as a prank by group of adolescent girls.
   b. 20 people executed. Hundreds imprisoned.
   c. Dramatized in the 20th Century as *The Crucible* by **Arthur Miller**.

1696 **The Board of Trade and Plantations**, the chief organ of **British** government with respect to the **American Colonies**, is established.

1702
1. **Queen Anne's War** begins.
   a. a.k.a., **The War of the Spanish Succession.**
   b. Although placing a heavy economic burden on colonies, has less effect than King William's War.
   c. Ends in 1713 with *Treaty of Utrecht*.

1711
1. **Tuscarora War** begins in NC.
   a. **Tuscarora** Indians were trading members of other tribes as slaves.
   b. These tribes joined **English** to fight against them.
   c. Ends in 1715.

1715
1. **Yamasee War** in South Carolina (SC) is a protest against English mistreatment and slavery.
   a. Ends in 1717.

1732 **Georgia (GA)** is chartered.

A Country Grows 1690-1771

1690 **John Locke** writes *Essay Concerning Human Understanding*, a major contribution to the era known as **"The Enlightenment."**

1691 **Massachusetts Bay Colony** gets a new charter; **Plymouth Colony, Nantucket, Maine (ME), Martha's Vineyard, Nova Scotia** are absorbed into it.

1693 **The College of William and Mary** is founded in the **Virginia Colony.**

1695 The city of **Annapolis** is laid out in MD to serve as the colonial capital.

1701 The city of **Detroit** is founded as the **French** settlement **Fort Pontchartrain** on a strait between **Lake Erie and Lake St. Clair.**

1721
1. **Smallpox** epidemic hits Boston.
   a. **Cotton Mather** urges citizens to try new medical procedure called "inoculation."
   b. Those who got inoculated survive in five times greater numbers.

1738 **George Whitefield** arrives in America and spreads the teachings of **"The Great Awakening."**

1739
1. Slaves in the **Stono River** area of SC arm themselves and rebel.
   a. Head for FL hoping for refuge in Spanish Colony.
   b. Militia puts down rebellion in a day.
   c. All blacks involved are killed immediately or executed subsequently.
   d. **Stono Rebellion** feeds fears of whites against black uprising and leads to a reign of terror in NY against imagined "conspirators."
2. **King George's War** (a.k.a., **War of the Austrian Succession)** begins with Spain.
   a. Ends in 1748.

1767
1. **"Regulator"** movement starts in SC.
   a. Essentially a "vigilante" movement against perceived lax law enforcement.
   b. Will spawn a "Regulator" movement in NC.

1769 SC Regulator movement ends.

1770 21-year-old Boston printer **Isaiah Thomas** begins publication of *The Massachusetts Spy*, one of the earliest pro-colonist/anti-British newspapers.

1771 NC movement ends in fierce battle between Regulators and militia at the **Battle of Alamance.**

Revolutionary Ideas 1754-1774

1754
1. **Albany Congress** is convened by delegates from seven **British** northern and middle colonies in response to **French** activities on the western frontiers.
   a. It attempts to convince **Iroquois** to abandon neutrality and join British, and to coordinate colonial defenses.
   b. Both goals fail.
2. **French and Indian War** begins (not officially declared until 1756).

1760
1. British dismissal of abilities of colonial soldiers in the French and Indian War leads to a furthering of dissension between **Colonies** and home country.
2. **George III** becomes King of England.

1763
1. *Treaty of Paris* is signed. France cedes all major North American holdings to England; Spain cedes FL.
2. **Pontiac**, war chief of an **Ottowa** village near Detroit, unites tribes and lays siege to a Detroit fort while his troops attack other British outposts in the region—a protest against encroaching British rule.
3. *Proclamation of 1763*, in effect, "apologizes" to the **Indians** for encroachment and declares a strict, temporary, boundary for colonial settlement.

1764 *Sugar Act*, designed specifically to enrich England, raises new duties on imports to the New World, infuriating the **Colonists.**

1765
1. *Stamp Act* imposes a heavy tax on Colonies.
   a. **"Sons of Liberty"** formed to unite colonials in opposition to the taxes. Some protests get violent.

1766 *Stamp Act* is repealed, but *Declaratory Act* asserts Britain's ability to tax and legislate for **American** possessions *"in all cases whatsoever."*

1767 *Townshend Acts* impose larger taxes on Colonies.

1770
1. **Lord North** becomes Prime Minister of Britain.
2. *Townshend Acts* are repealed ... except **tax on tea.**
3. **Boston Massacre** lights the fuse on American resentment at its highest.

1772 **Boston Committee of Correspondence** is formed and urges an immediate boycott of all British goods.

1773 *Tea Act* eliminates colonial middlemen, and profits to them, from tea trade. Colonial reaction leads directly to **Boston Tea Party.**

1774 *Coercive Acts*, better known as "*Intolerable Acts*," are implemented by **Lord North**, fanning the fire of revolution.

The Revolution 1774-1783

1774 First **Continental Congress** is convened.

1775
1. **Lord Dunmore's** *Proclamation* is issued.
   a. In a letter to **General Thomas Gage**, Dunmore downplays any chance of significant revolution from *"rude rabble without a plan."*
2. **Battles of Lexington and Concord** are fought; **Revolutionary War** officially begins.
3. **Second Continental Congress** is convened. Originally intended as "interim," it becomes, in essence, the colonial seat of government.

1776
1. **Thomas Paine** writes *Common Sense*, rallying **Colonists.**
2. The **British** evacuate Boston.
3. **Thomas Jefferson** drafts, and the Continental Congress signs, **The Declaration of Independence**; anti-slavery clauses omitted due to **Southern** pressure.
4. **Battle of New York** is fought.
   a. **General George Washington** proves a formidable foe.
   b. Delays on British side add to Colonists' strength.

1777
1. The British capture Philadelphia.
2. **British General John Burgoyne** surrenders at Saratoga (NY).

1778
1. France joins the battle on the Colonists' side.
2. The British evacuate Philadelphia.

QuickStudy®

The Road West - To War 1846-1861

1846
1. **Mexican-American War** begins over TX borders and lands west that President **James Polk** wants for U.S.
2. Representative **David Wilmot (D-PA.)** offers an amendment to a war appropriations bill: *"... neither slavery nor involuntary servitude shall ever exist..."* in territories won from Mexico. It fails but becomes the rallying cry for **"Free Soilers"** and abolitionists.

1847 Presidential candidate **General Lewis Cass (D)** proposes ***popular sovereignty*** (each territory to decide whether to be "slave" or "free").

1848 **Zachary Taylor** is elected President.

1849 CA applies for admission to the U.S.

1850 *Compromise of 1850*, devised by **Senators Henry ("The Great Compromiser") Clay** and **Stephen A. ("The Little Giant") Douglas**, admits CA as a free state, gives NM and UT territories power to legislate *"all rightful subjects...consistent with the Constitution"* (i.e., slavery), and promises stronger fugitive slave laws and suppression of slave trade in the **District of Columbia.**

1852
1. **Harriet Beecher Stowe's** *Uncle Tom's Cabin* is published and influences anti-slavery feelings. Abraham Lincoln will call Stowe "the little lady who started the war."
2. **Franklin Pierce** is elected President.

1854
1. *Kansas-Nebraska Act* repeals slavery limitations set by the *Missouri Compromise*, allowing Kansas (KS) and NE territories to be slave-owning if they so choose.
   a. Battles over **slavery** in KS earn it the nickname **"Bleeding Kansas."**
2. **Republican Party** is formed and makes inroads against the **Democrats** in congressional elections.

1857
1. ***Dred Scott v. Sanford*** effectively voids the *Missouri Compromise*.
   a. Scott, a Missouri (MO) slave, had sued for freedom, stating that he had been taken so frequently into free territory that he was a resident there.
   b. **Supreme Court** rules Scott *"not a citizen"*; therefore, not free; and, in any event, Congress could not bar slavery from a territory.
2. *Lecompton Constitution* (KS) permits slavery. It is defeated in 1858 after anti-slavery forces are elected to the majority.

1858
1. Senatorial candidate **Stephen A. Douglas (D-IL)** begins a series of cross-country debates with fellow candidate **Abraham Lincoln (R-IL).**
   a. Douglas' *Freeport Doctrine* states that territorial legislatures can bar slavery either by passing such a law or not enforcing slavery laws.
2. *The Yellow Rose of Texas*, written in 1836, is copyrighted.
3. **Iowa State College** and **Oregon State University** are founded.

1859 Abolitionist **John Brown** stages raid on **Harpers Ferry** (VA) in hopes of starting **slave revolt.** It fails.

1860
1. **Democratic Party** splits. **Southern** members walk out of the nominating convention to protest Douglas' mollifying "free" states.
2. **Abraham Lincoln** is elected President.
3. *Crittenden Compromise*, proposal to resolve secession crisis, **fails.**
4. **SC secedes** from the Union.

1861
1. MS, FL, AL, GA, LA, TX, VA, Arkansas (AR), NC and Tenessee (TN) all join SC in seceding.
   a. Together, they form the **Confederate States of America** (CSA).
   b. **Jefferson Davis** elected President.
2. KS enters the Union as a free state.
3. Abraham Lincoln sends a supply ship into SC territorial waters to bring food to **Fort Sumter** in **Charleston Harbor.**
   a. Given a choice between an attack on the fort or submission, the **Carolinians** attack.
4. **Civil War** (a.k.a., "War between the States") begins.

The Civil War 1861-1865

1861
1. **Battle of Bull Run**, named for a stream near **Manassas Junction (VA)**, shows that the war is very real and bloody.
   a. South wins when 9,000 additional troops under **General Thomas "Stonewall" Jackson** arrive.
   b. Many Southerners refer to battle as the first **Battle of Manassas.**
2. **General George McClellan** organizes an expanded **Union Army.**
3. Union blockade of confederate ports begins.
4. The first *Confiscation Act* is passed, allowing seizure of all "property" used for insurrection purposes, including slaves.
5. Detective **Allen Pinkerton** uncovers a plot to assassinate **Abraham Lincoln**, who hires him to form a "secret service" (later becomes **U.S. Secret Service**).

1862
1. **Forts Henry** and **Donelson** are captured by Union troops under **Ulysses S. Grant**, opening a major southern route to Mississippi Valley.
2. Confederates convert Union frigate *U.S.S. Merrimack* into iron-sided ship, renamed *C.S.S. Virginia*.
   a. In first battle between ironclad ships, *U.S.S. Monitor* fights *Virginia* to a draw.
   b. Forever changes naval warfare, as ironclads make wooden ships obsolete.
3. **New Orleans** is captured.
4. **Battle of Shiloh**, the bloodiest battle of the war thus far, is fought, altering perceptions of a "short" war.
   a. More than 1,700 are dead on each side.
   b. The battle is a Union victory.
5. **The Confederacy** is forced to adopt a draft.
6. McClellan attacks VA.
   a. Led by **General Robert E. Lee**, Confederate troops hold off the Union forces.
   b. Buoyed by this, **Jefferson Davis** orders his troops on the offensive.
7. Second *Confiscation Act* orders taking of property of all who support rebellion, even if that "support" is merely living in the south and paying taxes.
8. **Battle of Antietam** leads Lincoln to announce emancipation of all slaves in states whose people *"shall then be in rebellion against the United States"* on January 1, 1863 (*Emancipation Proclamation*).

1863
1. *National Banking Act* passed to raise money for Union.
2. The Union adopts a draft.
3. Black soldiers are allowed to join the Union Army. Many remain in service after the war and go west. The Indians call them **"Buffalo soldiers,"** as their dark skin, and tenacity in battle, is like fierce buffalo.
4. Blockade leads to food riots in many southern cities.
5. **Battle of Chancellorsville** (VA) is a surprise victory for the Confederacy over larger Union forces, thanks to the strategy of **Lee** and **Jackson.**
6. **Battle of Gettysburg** (PA): A disaster for the Confederacy; Lee's strategy is blamed. More than 7,000 are dead on both sides. Union: 3,000+ dead and 14,000+ wounded; Confederacy: 4,000+ dead and 12,000+ wounded. Battle marks turning point in the war.
7. **Vicksburg** (MS) surrenders.
8. Riots in NY protest the draft.
9. Congress refuses seating of **Southern Delegates.**

1864
1. In the **Battle of Cold Harbor** (VA), Grant loses over 12,000 men in just a few hours, but vows to fight it out *"...if it takes all summer."*
2. Lincoln requests a **Republican Party** platform abolishing slavery nationwide for upcoming election.
3. Union **General William Tecumseh Sherman** enters Atlanta.
4. Lincoln is re-elected.
5. Jefferson Davis proposes freeing and arming Confederate slaves.
6. Sherman's **March to the Sea** in GA decimates the countryside. His "scorched earth" policy of burning crops and property leaves nothing in its wake.

1865
1. Sherman continues his drive through the Carolinas.
2. The **13th Amendment** abolishes slavery.
3. **Hampton Roads Conference** (VA) is unsuccessful attempt to end war 2 months prior to Lee's surrender.
4. **General Robert E. Lee** surrenders to **General Ulysses S. Grant** at **Appomattox Courthouse** (VA).
5. **John Wilkes Booth** assassinates **Lincoln** in **Ford's Theater.**
   a. **Andrew Johnson** becomes President.

1865 (cont.)
6. Jefferson Davis **is captured**, and remaining Confederate forces lay down their arms.
7. **The war ends.** Union has lost 360,000 men; Confederacy, 258,000; both sides have 412,000+ wounded.

Reconstruction 1865-1877

1865
1. President **Andrew Johnson** continues **Reconstruction** begun by **Abraham Lincoln.**
2. *Black Codes* **enacted.**
3. **13th Amendment** ratified.

1866 **14th Amendment** passed, to apply civil rights, as guaranteed by **Bill of Rights**, to all states. It is rejected by **Southern** states.

1867
1. *Military Reconstruction Act* is passed.
2. *Tenure of Office Act* is passed.

1868
1. **Impeachment/acquittal** of Andrew Johnson.
2. **Readmission** of some Southern states begins.
3. **14th Amendment** ratified.
4. **Ulysses S. Grant** is elected President.
5. Amnesty declared for Confederates not indicted for treason or felonies; ***no amnesty*** for **Jefferson Davis.**

1870
1. The **15th Amendment** bars denying voting rights *"on account of race, color, or previous condition of servitude."*
2. *First Enforcement Act* is passed.

1871
1. *Ku Klux Klan Act* is passed.
2. *Second Enforcement Act* is passed.
3. *Treaty of Washington*, designed to settle questions of Canada/U.S. border rights, claims against Britain for damage to the **Confederate** ship *Alabama*, and some **North Atlantic** fishing rights, is signed.

1872
1. *Amnesty Act* is passed.
2. Debtors want greenbacks to remain as legal currency.
3. Grant elected to second term.

1873
1. **Panic of 1873.**
2. Congress makes gold sole monetary standard.

1874
1. Grant refuses to increase paper money supply.
2. Democrats become House majority.

1875
1. Corruption indictment of Grant appointees.
2. Passage of new *Civil Rights Act*.
3. **"Greenbacks"** (paper money) to be converted to gold by 1879.

1876
1. ***U.S. v. Reese:*** Constitution *"does not guarantee right to vote."*
2. ***U.S. v. Cruikshank:*** U.S. has no right to intervene in private discrimination.

1877 Congress elects **Rutherford B. Hayes President** after disputes in general election lead many to believe **Samuel Tilden** is winner.

American Innovation 1857-1877

1857 NY and St. Louis are connected by rail.

1858
1. **George M. Pullman** puts sleeping cars on trains.
2. **Ladies Christian Assoc.**, later **YWCA**, is formed.

1859 The first intercollegiate **baseball game** is played.

1860 **The Pony Express** is started. It ends in 1862, made unnecessary when **telegraph** lines reach CA.

1861 **Yale** grants the country's first **Ph.D.**

1862 First enclosed baseball field opens in **Brooklyn, NY.**

1864
1. *"In God We Trust"* appears on U.S. coins.
2. Trade unionism grows with organization of the **Cigar Makers** and **Brotherhood of Railway Locomotive Engineers**, one of the earliest labor unions.

1866 Congress authorizes the coining of the nickel.

1868 For federal employees, **8-hour workday** becomes law.

1869 First **transcontinental railroad** is completed (joining of **Union Pacific** and **Central Pacific**).

1870
1. **National Weather Bureau** is established.
2. The first black senator, **Hiram R. Revels**, is seated.

1871
1. **"Greenbacks"** (paper money) established as legal tender.
2. **Chicago fire** decimates much of the [illegible]

1873 Plagues of grasshoppers devastate Midw[illegible]nds.

1874 The first **bridge** to span the Mississipp[illegible]ned.

1875 "Osteopathy" developed by **Dr. Andr**[illegible]

1876 The first **National League baseball** [illegible]ed.

1877 **George B. Selden** makes 1-cylinder internal-combustion engine.

U.S. $4.95

ISBN-13: 978-142320847-1
ISBN-10: 142320847-1

50495

9 781423 208471

Customer Hotline #
1.800.230.9522

free downloads &
hundreds of titles at
quickstudy.com

6 54614 00847

The Revolution 1774-1783 *(continued)*

1779	**General John Sullivan** leads an expedition against the **Iroquois** for their support of British forces, which destroy all crops, orchards, and settlements.
1780	British control Charleston (SC).
1781	**General Charles Cornwallis** surrenders at Yorktown.
1782	Peace negotiations begin in Paris.
1783	*Treaty of Paris* gives the **Colonies** unconditional independence and establishes boundaries of the new country (later, the **United States of America**), while ignoring territorial claims of native tribes.

A Nation Is Formed 1776-1795

1776	1. **Second Continental Congress** directs each state to draft an individual constitution. 2. NC extends its jurisdiction by annexing the **Watauga** settlement, now calling it **Washington County.**
1777	1. *Articles of Confederation* forming the "united" states are sent to the states for ratification. 2. New Connecticut "republic" renames itself **Vermont (VT)**, and adopts a constitution mandating suffrage for all men and banning slavery.
1778	**Sandwich Islands**, later to become the state of **Hawaii (HI)**, are discovered by **Captain James Cook.**
1779	The first planting and use of sweet corn (from Indian tribe along **Susquehanna River**) occurs.
1780	To control rampant inflation, **Congress** passes the *40 to 1 Act*, stating that continental paper money will be redeemed at one-fortieth of its face value.
1781	*Articles of Confederation* are **ratified**.
1782	Congress adopts the **Great Seal** of the United States.
1783	1. **George Washington** issues his *Farewell Address* to the **Army**, and all troops are formally discharged. 2. **Noah Webster** publishes *Webster's Spelling Book*, codifying **American** words and spelling for the first time. a. First of a 3-book cycle entitled *A Grammatical Institute of the English Language, Comprising an Easy, Concise and Systematic Method of Education, Designed for the Use of English Schools in America.* b. In 1828, Webster will publish *An American Dictionary of the English Language.*
1785	1. **Acadians** settle in Louisiana (LA) where, combining their style of cookery with the native "injun," they become known as **Cajuns**. a. The **Great Expulsion of 1755** removed the Acadians from the Canadian Maritime provinces, scattering them along the eastern coast of North America, from Nova Scotia southward to GA. 2. Congress establishes the **dollar** as the **official U.S. currency**, using a decimal system devised by **Thomas Jefferson.**
1786	1. **Annapolis Convention** is held to discuss U.S. trade policies. a. 9 states name representatives but only 5 attend. b. Another convention called for in Philadelphia in 9 months. 2. Farmer **Daniel Shays** leads a rebellion against high taxes and low money supply in western MA. Because Shays and many others involved are "gentlemen" (i.e., landowners), government is forced to rethink policies.
1787	1. *Northwest Ordinance* guarantees settlers in the Northwest Territory many of the freedoms later to be incorporated into **Bill of Rights.** 2. **Constitutional Convention** convenes. a. The **Constitution** of the United States is signed on September 17. b. **Benjamin Franklin** states: *"...there are several parts of the constitution [sic] which I do not... approve (but) I expect no better and I am not sure that it is not the best."*
1788	1. **James Madison, John Jay,** and **Alexander Hamilton** urge NY's (and the nation's) ratification of the **Constitution** in the publication *The Federalist*, which explains the meaning of the Constitution and assures immediate addition of **Bill of Rights.** 2. The **Constitution** is **ratified.**
1789	**United States House of Representatives** holds its first meeting on April 1, 30 days before **George Washington** assumes the office of **President.**
1790	The first successful U.S. **cotton mill** is established in what will later become Pawtucket, RI.
1791	**Bill of Rights** becomes U.S. law with VA's ratification.
1793	President Washington meets, at his home, with the heads of his Departments of State, Treasury, and War, the Attorney General and the Postmaster General, thereby holding the **first "cabinet"** meeting.
1794	1. **Eli Whitney** invents the cotton gin. 2. **Battle of Fallen Timbers** (Ohio [OH]), led by **General "Mad" Anthony Wayne**, defeats native tribes demanding territorial rights and opens way for negotiations on settlement of the area.
1795	*Treaty of Greenville*, signed by Wayne and delegates from various native tribes, gives U.S. right to settle the **Ohio Territory**.

The Early Republic 1789-1800

1789	1. *Judiciary Act* provides for a **Supreme Court** of 6 members, including a **Chief Justice** and 5 associate justices. a. Defines jurisdiction of the federal judiciary. b. Establishes 13 district courts and 3 circuit courts of appeal. 2. **French Revolution** begins. 3. **Congress** passes the first *Tariff Act.* 4. **Georgetown University** has its beginnings. 5. First **American advertisement** for **tobacco** appears. 6. Baptist minister **Elijah Craig** distills the first bourbon whiskey in the Kentucky (KY) region.
1790	1. Secretary of the Treasury **Alexander Hamilton** issues the first *Report on Public Credit,* aiming to expand financial reach of federal government and reduce power of the states. 2. The **House of Representatives** votes to locate the nation's **capital** on a 10-mile stretch along the **Potomac River.** 3. Congress establishes **U.S. Patent Office.**
1791	1. **Bill of Rights** (first **10 amendments** to **Constitution**) ratified. 2. **VT** becomes the 14th state to enter the union. 3. **Thomas Paine** publishes *The Rights of Man,* arguing that power should rest with the democratic majority.
1793	1. France declares war on Britain, Spain, and Holland. U.S. remains neutral. 2. **Democratic-Republican Societies**, sympathetic to **French** cause, are founded. 3. **Thomas Jefferson** resigns as Secretary of State to head the anti-Federalist **Democratic-Republican Party.**
1794	1. The **Whiskey Rebellion** against high taxes leads **George Washington** to send troops to PA to avoid repeat of **Shays Rebellion.** 2. America's first trade union, **The Federal Society of Journeymen Cordwainers** (shoemakers), is organized.
1795	1. The *Jay Treaty* resolves issues of **Anglo-American** affairs, averting war. 2. **First railroad** in America, a wooden railed tramway running the slope of **Beacon Hill,** is built in Boston.
1796	1. **John Adams (Federalist)** is elected President; **Thomas Jefferson (Democratic-Republican)** is Vice President. 2. The Supreme Court rules on the constitutionality of an act of Congress for the first time, ***Hylton v. United States.*** 3. Congress passes the *Public Land Act*, providing liberal credit terms for land purchase and encouraging speculation in real estate and expansion. a. Superseded by the *Harrison Land Act* in 1800.
1797	First ship of the **United States Navy**, called, appropriately, the *United States*, is launched.
1798	1. **"XYZ Affair"** shows France treating America with disdain, leads to wave of anti-French sentiment. 2. *Alien and Sedition Acts,* four laws designed by Federalists to prevent dissent and the growth of Democratic-Republican Party (which supports France), are passed. 3. *Virginia and Kentucky Resolutions* repudiate the *Alien and Sedition Acts.* 4. Congress establishes the **Marine Hospital Service**, which later becomes the **U.S. Public Health Service.** 5. **Eli Whitney** pioneers the **"American System"** of **mass production** to build firearms. 6. U.S. and France engage in undeclared war in the West Indies (a.k.a., **The Quasi-War**).
1799	1. **George Washington dies.** a. **General Henry ("Lighthorse Harry") Lee** delivers a eulogy declaring Washington *"First in war, first in peace, and first in the hearts of his countrymen."*
1800	1. **Franco-American Convention** ends the Quasi-War and frees U.S. from obligations to France from the *Treaty of 1778.* 2. **Thomas Jefferson** is elected President; **Aaron Burr** is Vice President.
1800 *(cont.)*	3. **Second Great Awakening**, a wave of revivalism, provides religious fervor and revolutionary zeal to many women. 4. **Gabriel's Rebellion**, a black revolt in VA led by **Gabriel Prosser**, where the participants demand equal rights.

America Strengthens 1801-1823

1801	1. **Thomas Jefferson** is inaugurated. 2. **John Marshall** named Chief Justice of the Supreme Court.
1803	1. ***Marbury v. Madison*** establishes the Supreme Court's power to judge constitutionality of issues. 2. **Louisiana Purchase**, 828,000 square miles, expands U.S. territories westward, doubling the size of the country.
1804	1. Thomas Jefferson is re-elected. 2. **Lewis and Clark** expedition begins.
1806	Lewis and Clark expedition ends with information on vast territories in the Northwest.
1807	1. **Chesapeake Affair** exposes U.S. military weakness, as **British** ship attacks U.S. ship *Chesapeake* within U.S. territorial waters, seizing sailors and cargo. 2. *Embargo Act* forbids all U.S. exports and virtually eliminates imports.
1808	**James Madison** is elected President.
1812	**War of 1812** begins with the British.
1814	1. *Treaty of Ghent* on **Christmas Eve** halts hostilities. 2. **Hartford Convention** sees conservative **Federalists** opposing War of 1812 call for secession.
1815	**General Andrew Jackson** becomes a hero at **Battle of New Orleans.** Fought *after* the war had officially ended (unbeknownst to Jackson).
1816	1. **James Monroe** is elected President. 2. **Second Bank of the United States** is chartered.
1817	*Rush-Bagot Treaty* with Britain establishes size and number of naval vessels on American lakes.
1819	1. In ***McCulloch v. Maryland,*** Chief Justice John Marshall establishes that the Supreme Court supersedes state courts in matters of federal rights. 2. *Adams-Onis Treaty* cedes FL to the U.S. and sets U.S. southern border.
1820	1. *Missouri Compromise* **prohibits slavery** in Louisiana Territory states north of Missouri's (MO) southern boundary. 2. Monroe is re-elected.
1823	*Monroe Doctrine* declares *"most of the Western Hemisphere"* off-limits to foreign **(European)** intervention.

Looking at Life 1655-1806

1655	**Lady Deborah Moody** is the first woman granted a town charter (for Gravesend).
1673	**First mail service** is established between Boston and NY.
1700	**First publicly supported library** is established in Charleston.
1701	6 women sit on a jury in Albany (NY), denoting growing respect for women in public life.
1704	The first regularly published newspaper, *Boston News-Letter*, is published by **John Campbell.**
1714	Tea is introduced to the Colonies.
1729	**Benjamin Franklin** begins publishing what will become *The Saturday Evening Post.*
1734	**John Peter Zenger** is imprisoned for 8 months because of "seditious libels" (i.e., stories not to the liking of the established authority) in his newspaper.
1735	Zenger's paper endorses the **Popular Party** candidates for alderman; they win.
1737	The first celebration of **St. Patrick's Day** is held in Boston.
1789	1. **Society of Saint Tammany** is established in NY. It will become the epitome of power politics in the U.S. 2. **George Washington** calls for a day of "national thanksgiving" for victory in **Revolutionary War.**
1790	*Dobson's Encyclopedia*, an **American** version of the *Encyclopedia Britannica*, is published.
1793	The cornerstone is laid for the new **Capitol Building** on the **Potomac River.**
1800	Congress authorizes franking privileges (free postage) for **Martha Washington** and for **Revolutionary War** veterans.
1806	**Washington Irving** publishes his first stories and establishes the **Knickerbocker School of Authentically American Writing.**

Industry Grows 1807-1857

1807	**Robert Fulton** presents first steamboat, the *Clermont.*
1813	1. **Boston Manufacturing Company** is founded. a. Uses the first **American** power loom, which radically changes textile manufacturing. b. Combines all manufacturing processes under one roof.
1818	**National Pike** (a.k.a., **Cumberland Road**), a stone-based, gravel top highway beginning in Cumberland, MD, reaches Wheeling, VA (present-day West Virginia [WV]). It will reach Columbus (OH) by 1833.
1819	***Dartmouth College v. Woodward*** establishes non-interference by states in commerce and business where a "contract" exists.
1820	New England textile mills expand, dominating the market for decades.
1824	***Gibbons v. Ogden:*** Supreme Court ends monopoly on steamboat trade by ruling that Congress, not individual states, controls commerce as per the "commerce clause" of the Constitution.
1825	**Erie Canal** is completed.
1830	**Baltimore & Ohio Railroad** starts operating.
1831	**Cyrus McCormick** invents the **McCormick Reaper,** vastly improving farm productivity and efficiency.
1837	1. ***Charles River Bridge v. Warren Bridge*** establishes that new enterprises cannot be restricted by implied privileges under old charters which they were not party to. 2. An economic depression begins, lasting until 1843.
1844	Baltimore-Washington **telegraph** line is established.
1848	The discovery of gold at **Sutter's Mill** (California [CA]) starts the great CA **"Gold Rush."**
1854	The railroad reaches the Mississippi River.
1857	A new depression begins.

Population & Migration 1805-1849

1805	**Shawnee Indian Chiefs Prophet** and **Tecumseh** emerge as leaders preaching a united front against U.S. encroachment and military might. They will align with **British** in **War of 1812.**
1810	New York City surpasses Philadelphia in population.
1813	Tecumseh dies, as does hope of a united front against U.S. treaty policies.
1819	*Indian Civilization Act* is passed, aimed at assimilating tribes into the white mainstream through government financial aid and boarding schools.
1823	1. **Catherine Beecher,** with help of **Mary Lyon,** establishes **Hartford Female Seminary** to teach young women to be teachers. a. Seen as an extension of women's "nurturing" role in society. b. Will establish teaching as the career expectation for educated women in the workplace.
1824	President **James Monroe** proposes **removal** of all **Indians** to lands **west** of the **Mississippi River,** an "honorable" move to assure Indians' right to dwell in peace.
1827	*Freedom's Journal*, first black weekly, begins publication.
1831	1. ***Cherokee Nation v. Georgia*** attempts to fight Monroe's removal policy through legal means. a. Chief Justice **John Marshall** rules that Indians are neither a foreign nation nor a state, and so have no standing in a federal court. 2. **Trail of Tears** begins when **Choctaw** tribe (Mississippi [MS] & Alabama [AL]) is forced to lands west of the Mississippi River. Expands to include **Cherokee** in 1838.
1832	1. Justice John Marshall clarifies his position regarding the Cherokee by stating that the **Indian Nation** is a distinct political community in which the *"laws of the state of GA can have no force."* a. Further, forbids **Georgians** from entering without permission or treaty privilege. b. This is ignored and the Trail of Tears continues.
1835	**Seminole War** erupts. Led by **Osceola**, the Seminoles will battle until 1842.
1845	A potato famine starts in Ireland, leading to mass **Irish** immigration.
1848	An abortive revolution in Germany is the impetus for **German** immigration.
1849	1. A theater riot erupts in NY. a. As theaters were the place where people of all classes and races mixed in the same building, they became the arenas for "class wars." b. This riot is culmination of many smaller ones starting as early as 1830.

Expansion & Reform 1825-1848

1825	1. The **House of Representatives** elects **John Quincy Adams** President. 2. Adams delivers the first presidential message to **Congress,** urging growth, reform, establishment of a national university system, and an astronomical observatory in Washington. 3. Fur trader **Pierre Cabanne** opens **trading post** on **Missouri River**, which will become **Omaha** (Nebraska [NE]). 4. **General Simon Perkins** founds **Akron (OH).**
1826	1. **American Society for the Promotion of Temperance** is founded to defeat **"demon rum."** 2. **Anti-Masonry** becomes an organized movement when disillusioned **Mason William Morgan** writes exposé *The Illustration of Masonry by One of the Fraternity Who Has Devoted Thirty Years to the Subject.* 3. The first overland journey to Southern CA leaves **Great Salt Lake** on August 22, arrives in San Diego on November 27. 4. **Gideon B. Smith** plants first Chinese mulberry trees in U.S., giving impetus to infant **silk** industry. 5. **Lyceum movement** led by **Josiah Holbrook** spreads interest in the arts, sciences, and "public issues" throughout the eastern U.S.
1827	**Creek Indians,** forced off their western GA lands, cede area to U.S.
1828	1. Passage of *Tariff of Abominations* later leads southern states to devise the *Doctrine of Nullification,* which will give states the right to overrule federal legislation in conflict with their own (1832). 2. **Andrew Jackson** is elected President. 3. **Delaware and Hudson Canal** opens to transport **PA coal** to ports in NY and New England.
1829	**American Society for Encouraging Settlement in Oregon (OR)** is established to promote territorial settlement.
1830	The **(Daniel) Webster-(Robert Y.) Hayne Debates** discuss the notion of nullification and the meaning of "union."
1831	1. *Liberator*, an anti-slavery journal, begins publication. 2. The first national **Anti-Mason Convention** is held.
1832	1. Andrew Jackson vetoes rechartering of the **Second Bank of the United States.** 2. Jackson re-elected President.
1833	Americans in **Texas (TX)** vote to separate from Mexico.
1834	1. The U.S. government demands **Seminoles** leave FL, as per an 1832 treaty. 2. **Whig Party** develops in opposition to Jackson (superseded by **Republican Party** in 1854).
1835	Mexico proclaims a unified constitution that abolishes slavery. U.S. citizens living in TX vote to secede rather than give up this right.
1836	1. **Republic of Texas** is established. To end public land monopoly of speculators and capitalists, the *Specie Circular* states that only specie (gold or silver) or VA land scrip is acceptable payment for land. 2. **Martin Van Buren** is elected President.
1837	1. A financial panic hits the U.S. 2. Tensions rise along the U.S./Canada border. 3. **Horace Mann** is named first head of the **Massachusetts Board of Education**, a position he will hold until 1848. 4. U.S. enters a depression that will last until 1843.
1838	**Underground Railroad** is organized by abolitionists to provide slaves an escape route to the North.
1840	**William Henry Harrison** (Whig Party) wins Presidency.
1841	1. Upon Harrison's death (after less than a month in office), **John Tyler** becomes President. 2. Missionaries report the "wonders" of the **Oregon Territory**, leading to **"Oregon Fever"** for expansion.
1843	**European** support for an independent TX causes U.S. interest in annexation.
1844	**James Polk** is elected President.
1845	**TX** gains statehood.
1847	1. **Mormons** arrive in Utah (UT) Territory. 2. First **Chinese** immigrants arrive in NY.
1848	1. **Women's Rights Convention** is held in Seneca Falls, NY. 2. New York becomes base for the **Cunard Steamship Line**, making it the center of European travel to and from NY. 3. **A telegraph** line opens from NY to Chicago. 4. The **Oneida Community**, the first communal society in the U.S., is formed in central NY.

Slavery 1712-1865

1712	1. A **black insurrection** is staged in NY; 21 blacks are executed. 2. **Pennsylvania Colony** enacts legislation banning the importation of slaves.
1713	England's **South Sea Company** is granted permission to import a limited number of slaves per year into the **Spanish** colonies of North America for a period of 25 years.
1716	**First black slaves** arrive in **French** territory of **Louisiana (LA).**
1724	French LA governor **Sieur de Bienville** establishes *Code Noir* to regulate treatment of blacks.
1725	Right to a separate black **Baptist** church granted in Williamsburg (VA).
1731	A **British** order prohibits implementing duty on imported slaves by the colonial legislatures.
1739	**Stono Rebellion** breaks out in SC.
1740	A planned revolt by Charleston (SC) slaves revealed; 50 slaves hanged.
1741	**New York City panic** based on (unfounded) fears of a black uprising leads to 18 blacks hanged, 14 blacks burned to death, and 70 banished.
1749	**Georgia Colony** revokes a prohibition against slavery, giving it legal recognition and starting the plantation system.
1772	In the ***Sommersett Case,*** Chief Justice **Lord Mansfield** declares a slave free the moment he sets foot on British soil.
1774	1. VA Statesman **George Mason** leads his state's opposition to slavery. a. Applies to importing slaves to more states, ***not*** to **freeing existing slaves.**
1775	1. **The Society of Friends** (a.k.a., **Quakers**) establish **Society for the Relief of Free Negroes Unlawfully Held in Bondage.** a. **Benjamin Franklin** becomes president of society (1787) and publishes anti-slavery pamphlet (1789).
1780	The PA legislature mandates the gradual abolition of slavery within the state.
1788	The MA legislature enacts bill making slave trade illegal.
1790	Quakers present the **first petition** calling for the ***abolition of slavery*** to Congress.
1792	Clergyman **David Rice** fails in his attempt to get the **Kentucky Constitutional Convention** to outlaw slavery.
1793	Congress enacts the *Fugitive Slave Act.*
1794	1. Congress bans slave trade with foreign nations. 2. **Haitian slave uprising** will lead to 1795 **slave revolt** in LA.
1799	NY passes a gradual emancipation law.
1808	Congress passes legislation forbidding foreign slave trade.
1816	Clergyman **Robert Finley** founds **The American Colonization Society** to resettle freed slaves in Africa. Establishes the **Republic of Liberia.**
1820	Congress makes trade in foreign slaves an *"act of piracy."*
1821	**Benjamin Lundy** publishes *The Genius of Universal Emancipation*, one of the earliest abolition journals.
1822	A planned slave revolt in Charleston (SC) by freed black **Denmark Vesey** is thwarted.
1836	The MA state supreme court frees any slave brought across the state border.
1838	**Frederick Douglass** escapes to freedom and becomes first "fugitive slave" lecturer speaking in America and abroad, and leading equal rights demonstrations.
1841	The **Supreme Court** rules that 53 black mutineers from the Spanish slave ship *Amistad*, who had been taken into U.S. custody, shall be free to return to Africa.
1845	*Narrative of the Life of Frederick Douglass* is published, followed by establishment of the newspaper *North Star* (1847).
1850	Practice of selling slaves to new, and "less comfortable," plantations further south along the **Mississippi River** causes **"sold down the river"** to enter language.
1859	1. GA passes a law banning wills or deeds granting freedom to slaves, and enacts legislation allowing any black indicted for vagrancy to be sold. 2. President **James Buchanan** opposes slave trade, yet bans searches of U.S. ships by British patrols, thus giving virtual immunity to continue the trade.
1862	Congress **abolishes slavery** in District of Columbia and U.S. Territories.
1863	*Emancipation Proclamation* **frees slaves *only*** in those states at war against the Union.
1865	**Civil War** ends. **13th Amendment**, freeing slaves in ***both*** North and South, is ratified.